TWELVE MARBLE QUESTIONS

TWELVE MARBLE QUESTIONS
*A Structural History of Greece
in Twelve Poems*

by J. A. Gucci
Teacher Edition

Pressure System Press
New York, New York

2026

Contents

How to Use This Book

This book presents Greek history through short poems organized around systems. Each poem models how systems interact, respond, and produce new forms over time.

The poems are not meant to be interpreted in the traditional literary sense. Instead, they function as representations of structure. Each poem corresponds to a triad of related elements (for example: Stone · Hill · Polis) that together describe how a system operates.

The goal is not to ask what a poem "means," but to examine what the system does.

Each poem is paired with notes that provide:

• historical context

• a correspondence between the poem and a historical system

• discussion prompts aligned to the triad

These materials support observation, comparison, and analysis across contexts.

The poems may be used in a variety of settings:

• as brief openings to introduce a topic

• as points of comparison alongside historical material

- as prompts for discussion of cause and effect

- as models for identifying interacting systems

Because the poems are concise and focused, they can be incorporated into a lesson, seminar, or independent study without replacing existing material. They are intended to clarify structure rather than add interpretive complexity.

Across the book, attention should be given to interaction and emergence. The systems presented here develop through the relationships between parts, producing outcomes that arise from collective behavior.

.

"All humans by nature desire to know."
— Aristotle

Instructor Notes

Poem Title: Double Helix
Triad: Stone · Hill · Polis

System Correspondence:

In ancient Greece, rocky terrain and steep hills shaped settlement patterns. Communities formed in isolated, elevated locations, leading to the development of independent city-states, or poleis. Geography produced separation, but also dense local organization.

In the poem, the opening structure—"sugared back-bones / yolked by a base— / twisted"—establishes stone as a repeating framework. The system begins with fixed structure and constraint.

The shift occurs through movement—"undulating waves, / streaks, / pulsing spheres—"—corresponding to hill: variation within the structure that introduces differentiation and interaction across parts.

The final image—"starlings"—corresponds to polis: an emergent system formed through the coordinated behavior of many individual units. In Greece, separate communities organized into bounded systems shaped by both constraint and interaction.

Discussion Prompts:

Stone: What role did physical geography play in shaping settlement patterns in ancient Greece?

Hill: How does variation in landscape influence how systems form and interact?

Polis: What forms of organization emerge when individual units coordinate within a constrained environment?

Double Helix

Sugar back-bones
twisted—
yolked by a base.

Undulating waves,
streaks,
pulsing spheres—

starlings.

Instructor Notes

Poem Title: Lotus
Triad: Sea · Ship · Exchange

System Correspondence:

In ancient Greece, the sea connected otherwise separated regions. Movement across water allowed goods, materials, and ideas to circulate between communities. These interactions formed networks of exchange that linked distant systems.

In the poem, the opening condition —" glass lake"— establishes sea as a continuous medium that enables movement. The system begins with a shared environment.

The shift occurs through interaction—"porous green / lotus—" —corresponding to ship: a bounded structure that moves within and engages the surrounding medium. The organism absorbs and releases material, functioning as a carrier within the system.

The final image—"bubbles"—corresponds to exchange: the transfer of material between systems. Input and output occur through interaction with the surrounding environment. In Greece, ships enabled similar exchanges, moving resources across the sea and connecting regions into a broader network.

Discussion Prompts:

Sea: What role does a shared medium play in connecting separate regions?

Ship: How do carriers enable movement within a system?

Exchange: What results when materials move between connected systems?

Lotus

Glass lake—
metallic glimmer.

Mayfly
drifting on a lotus—

bubbles.

Instructor Notes

Poem Title: Barnacle
Triad: Wall · Market · Citizen

System Correspondence:

In ancient Greece, city-states were defined by physical boundaries such as walls, which enclosed and protected the community. Within these boundaries, markets functioned as sites of interaction where goods, people, and ideas circulated. Citizens operated within this system, depending on continuous exchange.

In the poem, the opening condition—"granite cliffs, / sandy slopes—"—establishes wall as a fixed boundary that defines space. The system begins with separation between inside and outside.

The shift occurs through movement—"ebb, / flow—"—corresponding to market: continuous interaction at the boundary. Material and activity move across and along this edge.

The final image—"barnacles"—corresponds to citizen: units fixed within the system that depend on ongoing flow. The organism remains attached but relies on movement around it. In Greece, citizens were similarly embedded within the city, participating in and sustained by systems of exchange.

Discussion Prompts:

Wall: What role do boundaries play in defining and protecting a system?

Market: How does interaction at a boundary enable exchange?

Citizen: What forms of participation emerge within a system shaped by continuous interaction?

Barnacles

Granite cliffs,
sandy slopes—

ebb,
flow—

barnacles.

Instructor Notes

Poem Title: Cascade
Triad: Voice · Law · Assembly

System Correspondence:

In ancient Greece, political systems developed in which individuals could express ideas, but participation was structured by laws that shaped how decisions were made. Assemblies brought individuals together, producing collective outcomes through organized interaction.

In the poem, the opening condition—"scent of rain, / snorting zebra—"—establishes voice as an initiating signal. The system begins with input that prompts response.

The shift occurs through constraint—"dry grassland—"— corresponding to law: conditions that limit and structure possible actions. Movement is shaped by the environment rather than determined by any single unit.

The final image—"cascade"—corresponds to assembly: a collective outcome emerging from many individual responses. In Greece, assemblies functioned in this way, where individual voices operated within shared constraints to produce unified decisions.

Discussion Prompts:

Voice: What role do individual inputs play in initiating action within a system?

Law: How do constraints shape how individuals respond within a system?

Assembly: What forms of organization emerge when individual actions combine into a collective outcome?

Cascade

Petrichor,
zebra snort.

Dry
grassland—

cascade.

Instructor Notes

Poem Title: Imbrication
Triad: Shield · Spear · Phalanx

System Correspondence:

In ancient Greece, warfare was organized through the phalanx
—a tightly coordinated formation of soldiers equipped with
shields and spears. Each unit depended on others, creating a
system where strength emerged from alignment and
interdependence rather than individual action.

In the poem, the opening condition—"pitted plates— / ball
and socket / joints"—establishes shield as articulated
structure. The system begins with connected units capable of
coordinated movement.

The shift occurs through extension—"protruding spears— /
spine to spine—"—corresponding to spear: projection outward
from within the structure. Individual elements act, but only in
alignment with the whole.

The final term—"imbrication"—corresponds to phalanx: an
interlocking system in which units overlap and reinforce one
another. In Greece, this formation produced collective strength
through coordination and mutual dependence.

Discussion Prompts:

Shield: What role do individual units play within a
coordinated system?

Spear: How does projection or action depend on alignment
with others?

Phalanx: What results when units interlock to form a unified
structure?

Imbrication

Pitted plates,
ball and socket—

protruding spears,
spine to spine—

imbrication.

Instructor Notes

Poem Title: Mangrove
Triad: Sea · Trireme · Empire

System Correspondence:

In ancient Greece, control of the sea enabled movement beyond local territories. Ships such as triremes carried people, goods, and military force across the Mediterranean, connecting distant regions. Through repeated movement and settlement, networks expanded outward, extending influence across space.

In the poem, the opening condition—"eddies and gyres— / swirling, / undulating"—establishes sea as a dynamic medium of movement. The system begins with continuous flow that enables transport.

The shift occurs through a bounded unit—"buoyant seedling— / wing-beats—"—corresponding to trireme: a carrier moving within and across the system. The organism travels through the medium, maintaining structure while in motion.

The final image—"mangrove stand"—corresponds to empire: a system that expands by establishing new nodes of growth. Individual units take root and multiply, forming an extended network. In Greece, maritime movement produced similar patterns, where new settlements and connections extended influence outward.

Discussion Prompts:

Sea: What role does a moving medium play in enabling expansion?

Trireme: How do carriers extend movement across a system?

Empire: What results when systems spread by establishing new points of connection?

Mangrove

Eddies and gyres—
swirling,
undulating.

Buoyant seedling—
wing-beats—

mangrove stand.

Instructor Notes

Poem Title: Tectonic
Triad: Marble · Column · Temple

System Correspondence:

In ancient Greece, temples were constructed from carefully shaped stone, often marble, assembled into columns and structural systems. These buildings relied on precise alignment and the joining of individual parts to create stable, enduring forms.

In the poem, the opening condition—"hard pitted / brittle / white shafts—"—establishes marble as the base material. The system begins with dense, structured matter capable of bearing load.

The shift occurs through arrangement—"plates, / stacked—" —corresponding to column: the vertical organization of material into aligned support. Individual elements are positioned in relation to one another.

The final term—"tectonic"—corresponds to temple: a system formed through the joining of parts into a stable whole. Structure emerges from the relationships between components. In Greece, temples reflected this principle, where strength depended on the precise arrangement of material.

Discussion Prompts:

Marble: What properties make a material suitable for construction?

Column: How does the arrangement of parts create structural support?

Temple: What results when individual elements are organized into a unified system?

Tectonic

Hard pitted
brittle
white shafts—

plates,
stacked—

tectonic.

Instructor Notes

Poem Title: Waggle Dance
Triad: Chorus · Mask · Theatre

System Correspondence:

In ancient Greece, theatre developed as a structured system of
collective expression. The chorus provided a shared voice,
while actors used masks to assume roles and present different
identities. Performances took place within a defined space
where meaning emerged through coordinated action.

In the poem, the opening condition—"banana-tinted / rose
— / warm— / fermenting sugar / air"—establishes chorus as
a shared signal that gathers participants. The system begins
with an environment that attracts and organizes collective
attention.

The shift occurs through transformation—"dark throat, /
folded petals—"—corresponding to mask: entry into a
bounded space where identity is altered or concealed. The
structure shapes how participants appear and act.

The final image—"dusty waggle dance"—corresponds to
theatre: a system of performed communication. Movement
conveys information through coordinated action within a
shared space. In Greece, theatre functioned in this way, where
structured performance produced meaning for an audience.

Discussion Prompts:

Chorus: What role does a shared signal or voice play in
organizing collective attention?

Mask: How does transformation of identity affect participation
within a system?

Theatre: What results when meaning is produced through
coordinated performance?

Waggle Dance

Banana-tinted rose,
warm
fermenting sugar
air.

Sticky stem
tucked in a throat—
dark,
folded petals—

yellow waggle dance.

Instructor Notes

Poem Title: Succession
Triad: Problem · Reason · Philosophy

System Correspondence:

In ancient Greece, philosophy developed as a response to fundamental problems about the world, human life, and knowledge. Thinkers used reason to organize responses, gradually forming systems of thought that provided structured explanations.

In the poem, the opening condition—"blazing canopy—"—establishes problem: a disruption or breakdown of an existing system. The initial state is unstable and cannot continue as before.

The shift occurs through process—"grass, shrubs—"—corresponding to reason: a sequence of responses shaped by conditions. Growth follows a pattern, where each stage builds on what precedes it.

The final image—"hickory forest"—corresponds to philosophy: a stabilized system that emerges over time from repeated processes. Structure develops through accumulation and organization. In Greece, philosophical systems formed in this way, emerging from sustained reasoning in response to problems.

Discussion Prompts:

Problem: What role does disruption play in initiating new systems?

Reason: How do processes develop in response to changing conditions?

Philosophy: What results when responses become organized into stable systems of thought?

Succession

Blazing canopy—

spindly grass
shrubs—

hickory forest.

Instructor Notes

Poem Title: Wilt
Triad: Expansion · Strain · Instability

System Correspondence:

In ancient Greece, periods of expansion brought increased wealth, influence, and complexity. As systems grew, they placed strain on political structures, resources, and social organization. Continued pressure could lead to instability and breakdown.

In the poem, the opening condition—"swollen leaf / bowed outward—"—establishes expansion: growth beyond initial limits. The system increases in size and intensity.

The shift occurs through restriction—"shut pore—"—corresponding to strain: the system attempts to regulate itself under pressure. Internal mechanisms begin to fail or close.

The final image—"wilt"—corresponds to instability: loss of function following sustained strain. The system can no longer maintain balance. In Greece, expansion often produced pressures that contributed to internal weakening and disorder.

Discussion Prompts:

Expansion: What forms of growth can place pressure on a system?

Strain: How do systems respond when pushed beyond their limits?

Instability: What results when a system can no longer maintain balance?

Wilt

Swollen bowed
leaf—

collapsed pores—

wilt.

Instructor Notes

Poem Title: Brood Parasite
Triad: Citizen · Rivalry · Civil War

System Correspondence:

In ancient Greece, conflict did not occur only between city-states but also within them. Internal rivalries between groups or factions could weaken the structure of a society, leading to instability and, at times, civil war. These conflicts disrupted normal organization and could result in breakdown or abandonment.

In the poem, the opening condition—"eggs in a honeycomb / cell—"—establishes citizen: an ordered system of units organized within a shared structure. The system begins with stability and coordination.

The shift occurs through intrusion—"parasite— / eggs in a honeycomb—"—corresponding to rivalry: competing elements enter and disrupt the existing system. Order is challenged from within.

The final image—"empty stand"—corresponds to civil war: internal conflict that leads to collapse. The system is no longer able to sustain itself. In Greece, internal rivalries could produce similar outcomes, weakening or destroying the structures they depended on.

Discussion Prompts:

Citizen: How are individuals organized within a stable system?

Rivalry: How do competing internal forces disrupt an existing system?

Civil War: What results when conflict emerges from within a system rather than from outside it?

Brood Parasite

Eggs in a honeycomb—
eaten.

Parasite—
eggs in a honeycomb—

empty stand.

Instructor Notes

Poem Title: Nurse Log
Triad: Ruin · Fragment · Memory

System Correspondence:

In ancient Greece, the decline of systems led to the breakdown of structures and institutions. What remained were fragments —partial materials and traces of what once functioned as a whole. These remnants did not restore the system but preserved evidence of its prior form.

In the poem, the opening condition—"seed under log / wet in a pleat"—establishes fragment: a remnant held within the remains of a previous system. The system begins with what is left behind.

The shift occurs through interruption—"night white bloom— / frost—"—corresponding to ruin: conditions that prevent continuation. Growth is halted, and the system cannot sustain itself.

The final image—"ruptured— / woody ribs"—corresponds to memory: the persistence of structure as trace. What remains is not function, but form. In Greece, ruins and fragments served as records of prior systems, preserving their presence without restoring their operation.

Discussion Prompts:

Ruin: What processes lead to the breakdown of systems?

Fragment: What kinds of remains persist after a system collapses?

Memory: What results when a system survives only as trace rather than function?

Nurse Log

Seed under log
wet in a pleat.

Night white bloom—
frost—

ruptured—
woody ribs.

Guide to Use

This book presents Greek history through systems that develop through interaction. Each poem models how individual elements respond to one another, producing outcomes that emerge from collective behavior.

A typical use begins with close observation. The poem is read, and attention is directed toward condition, interaction, and result. From there, the corresponding system can be identified and connected to historical material.

The poems may be used in a variety of ways:

• to introduce a topic through an interacting system

• to accompany historical readings as a parallel model

• to support discussion of cause and effect

• to compare systems shaped by interaction

• to frame written or analytical responses

Because the poems are brief and focused, they can be incorporated into a lesson, seminar, or independent study without replacing existing material. They function as tools for recognizing relationships rather than as objects of interpretation.

Use may be adapted depending on context. The emphasis remains on identifying how parts interact, how responses are shaped, and how outcomes emerge from those interactions.

Curriculum Placement

Typical Course Placement

This book aligns with courses that examine ancient Greece, political systems, and the development of social and intellectual structures.

It may be used within secondary or introductory postsecondary courses, as well as in interdisciplinary contexts that focus on interaction, networks, and collective behavior.

Curriculum Connections

The poems correspond to major themes in Greek history:

- the formation and structure of the polis
- trade and exchange across the Mediterranean
- political participation and collective decision-making
- warfare and coordinated systems
- cultural practices such as theatre and philosophy
- expansion, conflict, and internal instability

Each poem models a system shaped by interaction, allowing readers to examine how relationships between elements produce outcomes over time.

The material supports analysis of cause and effect, comparison across systems, and the study of how complex societies emerge through coordinated activity.

Glossary

Imbrication — an overlapping arrangement of parts

Tectonic — the joining of parts into a stable structure

Waggle dance — a movement used by bees to communicate location

Brood parasite — an organism that lays its eggs in another's nest

Nurse log — a fallen tree that supports new growth

Stomata — openings on a leaf that regulate gas and water exchange

Gyre — a circular movement of water

Propagule — a plant structure capable of developing into a new organism

Pleat — a fold that creates a small pocket or space

Appendix

The Triad Method

The poems in this book are organized around triads —groups of three related elements that describe how a system operates.

Rather than presenting history as a sequence of events, the triads focus on relationships between conditions, interactions, and outcomes. Each triad represents a process: a system that forms, develops, or changes over time.

A triad may be understood as:

condition → what exists
interaction → how elements act upon one another
result → what emerges

The poems model these relationships using observable processes. The goal is not to interpret the poem, but to identify how the system functions.

This method can be applied beyond the book. Any system—historical, ecological, or social—can be examined by identifying three interacting elements that explain how it operates.

By focusing on structure rather than description, the triads provide a way to see how complex systems develop through interaction and produce new forms over time.

The Twelve Series

Each book in this series presents systems through short, structured poems.

Rather than describing events, the poems model how systems form, interact, and change over time.

Each volume focuses on a different civilization, using the same method to reveal how complex societies develop.

History

Mesopotamia — Formation
Greece — Interaction
Rome — Expansion and Collapse
Medieval — Thresholds

Creative Writing

Twelve Small Windows
Twelve Loops
Twelve Mirrors
Twelve Rooms

Philosophy

Twelve Iron Paradoxes.

About the Author

J. A. Gucci is an educator and writer whose work focuses on systems, structure, and the relationship between form and meaning.

His books present historical and conceptual material through short, structured poems designed to model how systems form and change over time

Colophon

This book was set in a clear, readable typeface to support close observation and sustained attention.

The poems follow a consistent structure to emphasize pattern, change, and system relationships.

Designed and produced as part of the Twelve series.